Land of Liberty

North Carolina

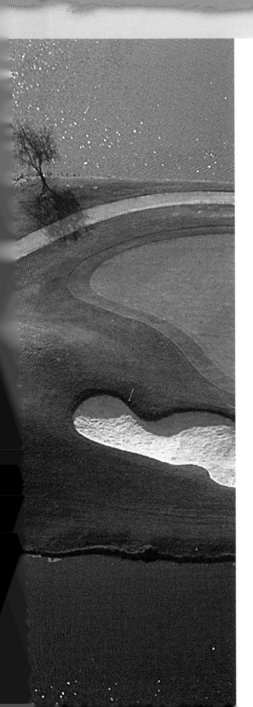

by Tracey Boraas

Consultant:
Janice Williams
Associate Director
North Carolina Museum of
History Division
Raleigh, North Carolina

Capstone
press
Mankato, Minnesota

Capstone Press
151 Good Counsel Drive • P.O. Box 669 • Mankato, Minnesota 56002
http://www.capstone-press.com

Library of Congress Cataloging-in-Publication Data
Boraas, Tracey.
    North Carolina / by Tracey Boraas.
    p. cm.—(Land of liberty)
    Summary: An introduction to the geography, history, government, politics,
economy, resources, people, and culture of North Carolina, including maps, charts,
and a recipe.
    Includes bibliographical references and index.
    ISBN 0-7368-2190-2 (hardcover)
    1. North Carolina—Juvenile literature. [1. North Carolina.] I. Title. II. Series.
F254.3.B67 2004
975.6—c21   2002154998

Editorial Credits
Angela Kaelberer, editor; Jennifer Schonborn, series designer; Molly Nei,
    book designer; Enoch Peterson, illustrator; Heather Atkinson, photo
    researcher; Eric Kudalis, product planning editor

Photo Credits
Cover images: Blue Ridge Parkway, photo courtesy of NC Division of Tourism,
    Film, and Sports Development; Charlotte skyline, Panoramic Images/Jerry
    Driendl Photography

Ann & Rob Simpson, 12–13; Capstone Press/Gary Sundermeyer, 54; Cherokee
Historical Association, 48; Corbis/Jack Moebes, 31; Richard A. Cooke, 41;
Courtesy of Army Art Collection, U.S. Army Center of Military History, 24;
Defense Visual Information Center, 27; Getty Images/Hulton Archive/NARA, 28;
Newsmakers/Alex Wong, 36; The Granger Collection, 22–23; North Wind Picture
Archives, 18, 58; One Mile Up Inc., 55 (both); Pat & Chuck Blackley, 57; Photo
courtesy of NC Division of Tourism, Film, and Sports Development, 1, 8, 14, 17,
44–45, 46, 50, 52–53, 63; Photo courtesy of The Fayetteville (NC) Observer, 43;
Photodisc, Inc. 56; Stock Montage, Inc., 21; UNICORN Stock Photos/Ann &
Rob Simpson, 4; Jean Higgins, 32; Audrey Gibson, 38; U.S. Postal Service, 59

Artistic Effects
Corbis; Image Ideas Inc.; North Carolina Division of Tourism; PhotoDisc

1 2 3 4 5 6 08 07 06 05 04 03

Table of Contents

Chapter 1   About North Carolina 5

Chapter 2   Land, Climate, and Wildlife 9

Chapter 3   History of North Carolina 19

Chapter 4   Government and Politics 33

Chapter 5   Economy and Resources 39

Chapter 6   People and Culture 47

Maps   North Carolina Cities 7
North Carolina's Land Features 11

Features   Recipe: Pig-Picking Cake 54
North Carolina's Flag and Seal 55
Almanac 56
Timeline 58
Words to Know 60
To Learn More 61
Internet Sites 61
Places to Write and Visit 62
Index 64

Cape Hatteras Lighthouse has stood in its present location since 1999.

Chapter 1

About North Carolina

Sandbars called barrier islands stretch along North Carolina's 301 miles (484 kilometers) of coast. The outermost barrier islands are called the Outer Banks. These sandbars form a natural wall between the mainland and the Atlantic Ocean. Cape Hatteras, Cape Lookout, and Cape Fear are places where the sandbars stretch far into the Atlantic Ocean.

In the 1600s and 1700s, pirates sailed around the Outer Banks. The pirates captured other ships. The pirates kidnapped or killed the passengers and stole their possessions.

Pirates no longer threaten the North Carolina coast. But the shifting sands of the Outer Banks are still dangerous. They form areas where the water suddenly becomes shallow. Cape Hatteras has been the site of hundreds of shipwrecks.

North Carolinians built lighthouses. These lighted towers warn ships of the dangerous waters. Cape Hatteras Lighthouse is the tallest brick lighthouse in North America. It is 198 feet (60 meters) tall.

Cape Hatteras Lighthouse was 1,500 feet (457 meters) away from the ocean when it was built in 1870. By 1935, water had worn away much of the sand. The lighthouse was then only 100 feet (30 meters) from the ocean. In 1999, the National Park Service moved the lighthouse to a new place 1,600 feet (488 meters) from the ocean.

The Tar Heel State

North Carolina is located in the southeastern United States. The Atlantic Ocean borders North Carolina to the east. The state is bordered by Virginia on the north and Tennessee on the west. Georgia and South Carolina lie to the south.

North Carolina's nickname is the Tar Heel State. Some people believe the name "Tar Heel" came from a story told during the Civil War (1861–1865). The story says that some Confederate troops ran away during a battle while North Carolina soldiers kept fighting. North Carolina soldiers threatened to put tar on the heels of the other Confederate soldiers. The tar would make the soldiers' feet stick to the ground and keep them from running away.

North Carolina Cities

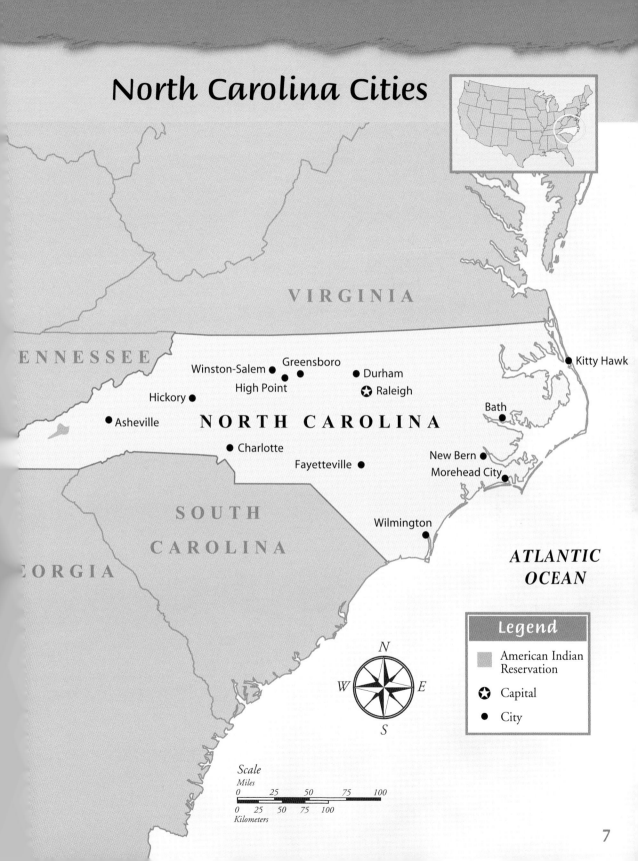

VIRGINIA

TENNESSEE

Winston-Salem • • Greensboro
High Point •
• Durham
☆ Raleigh

Hickory •

• Asheville

NORTH CAROLINA

• Charlotte

Fayetteville •

Kitty Hawk •

Bath •

New Bern •
Morehead City •

SOUTH

CAROLINA

Wilmington •

GEORGIA

ATLANTIC OCEAN

Legend	
	American Indian Reservation
☆	Capital
●	City

N
W   E
S

Scale
Miles
0   25   50   75   100
0 25 50 75 100
Kilometers

Whitewater Falls in the Mountain Region is one of the highest waterfalls in the eastern United States.

Chapter 2

Land, Climate, and Wildlife

North Carolina is divided into three main land regions. These areas are the Atlantic Coastal Plain, the Piedmont, and the Mountain Region.

Atlantic Coastal Plain

North Carolina's Atlantic Coastal Plain covers about 45 percent of the state. The plain spreads inland from the coast. The Dismal Swamp covers the northeastern corner of the region. The swamp is one of the largest in the United States. It is 37 miles (60 kilometers) long and up to 12 miles (19 kilometers) wide. Most of the swamp is in North Carolina. The rest is in Virginia.

Wetlands do not cover all of the Atlantic Coastal Plain. Rich farmland lies in the western part of the region. Sandy areas with well-drained soil are covered with pine forests.

Piedmont

The Piedmont is a hilly region that covers about 45 percent of the state. The land is about 300 feet (90 meters) above sea level in the eastern part of the region. The land slopes up to about 1,500 feet (457 meters) above sea level in the west.

The fall line forms a natural border between the Piedmont and the Coastal Plain. The fall line formed as streams and rivers washed away the soft soils of the Coastal Plain. The harder rock of the Piedmont left a rocky ledge. Rivers flow over this ledge to the Coastal Plain below. Nearly every river and stream in the fall line has rapids or waterfalls.

The sandy soil of the Sandhills covers the southeastern corner of the Piedmont. Golf courses, peach orchards, and horse farms are found in this area.

Mountain Region

North Carolina's Mountain Region covers the remaining 10 percent of the state. It forms a border between North

North Carolina's Land Features

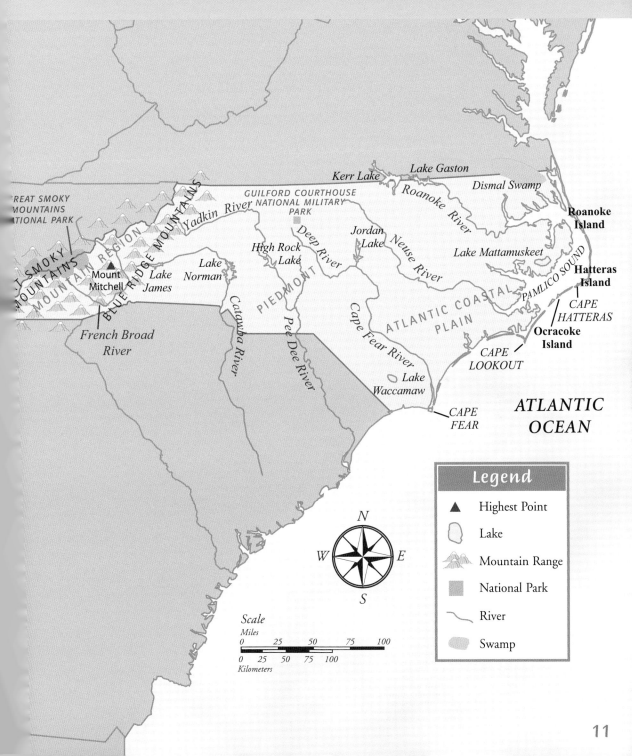

GREAT SMOKY MOUNTAINS NATIONAL PARK

GT. SMOKY MOUNTAINS

BLUE RIDGE MOUNTAINS

MOUNTAIN REGION

Mount Mitchell

Lake James

Lake Norman

French Broad River

Yadkin River

GUILFORD COURTHOUSE NATIONAL MILITARY PARK

High Rock Lake

Deep River

Jordan Lake

PIEDMONT

Catawba River

Pee Dee River

Cape Fear River

Lake Waccamaw

Kerr Lake

Lake Gaston

Roanoke River

Dismal Swamp

Roanoke Island

Neuse River

Lake Mattamuskeet

PAMLICO SOUND

Hatteras Island

CAPE HATTERAS

Ocracoke Island

ATLANTIC COASTAL PLAIN

CAPE LOOKOUT

CAPE FEAR

ATLANTIC OCEAN

Legend

▲	Highest Point
	Lake
	Mountain Range
	National Park
	River
	Swamp

N W E S

Scale

Miles

0   25   50   75   100

0   25   50   75   100

Kilometers

Carolina, Georgia, and Tennessee. The Blue Ridge Mountains are North Carolina's main mountain range. Smaller ranges include the Bald, Black, Great Smoky, and Unaka Mountains.

About 50 peaks in the Mountain Region are at least 6,000 feet (1,829 meters) high. In the Black Mountains, Mount Mitchell rises 6,684 feet (2,037 meters) above sea level. It is the highest peak in eastern North America.

Grandfather Mountain is the highest peak in the Blue Ridge Mountains. Some people think the mountain is shaped like the body of an old man. Grandfather Mountain is

5,964 feet (1,818 meters) high. It has a swinging bridge that is 1 mile (1.6 kilometers) above sea level. The bridge stretches across a space that is 228 feet (69 meters) long and 80 feet (24 meters) deep.

The name of the Great Smoky Mountains comes from the smoky blue mist that hangs over them. This mist is actually fog that covers the dark mountains. About 522,000 acres (211,000 hectares) of the mountains form Great Smoky Mountains National Park. Part of the park is in North Carolina. The other part is in Tennessee.

Many people enjoy the view from the Mile High Swinging Bridge on Grandfather Mountain. Built in 1952, the bridge is open only to foot traffic. In 1999, workers replaced the bridge's floor boards, side rails, and cables.

Rivers and Lakes

Most rivers in North Carolina begin in the Mountain and Piedmont regions and flow southeast. The 410-mile (660-kilometer) Roanoke River is one of the state's longest rivers. It begins in southern Virginia and flows across the northeastern corner of the state. It finally empties into Albemarle Sound. The Cape Fear River begins in the Piedmont and flows southeast through the Atlantic Coastal Plain. It empties into the Atlantic Ocean at Cape Fear. The Neuse and Tar Rivers drain the Piedmont as they flow into Pamlico Sound. The Yadkin River also begins in the central Piedmont. Near the South Carolina border, the Yadkin joins

The French Broad River forms rapids as it flows 210 miles (338 kilometers) from the North Carolina mountains into Tennessee.

with the Uharie River. Together they form the Pee Dee River. The Catawba River begins in McDowell County and joins with the Wateree in South Carolina.

The French Broad is one of several rivers that form west of the Continental Divide. They all end up draining into the Gulf of Mexico.

All of North Carolina's natural lakes are located on the Atlantic Coastal Plain. Lake Mattamuskeet is the largest. It covers about 90 square miles (233 square kilometers).

River dams formed most of North Carolina's lakes. The Kerr Dam on the Roanoke River created Kerr Lake, also called Buggs Island Lake. The 50,000-acre (20,235-hectare) lake stretches from southern Virginia into North Carolina. In the Piedmont, the Cowans Ford Dam formed Lake Norman. This lake covers 32,510 acres (13,157 hectares). It is the largest constructed lake completely within North Carolina.

Climate

North Carolina's climate varies with the region. The climates of the Atlantic Coastal Plain and the Piedmont are similar. Both summers and winters are warmer in these regions than in the Mountain Region. North Carolina receives an average of 49 inches (124 centimeters) of precipitation each year.

Hurricanes sometimes strike North Carolina. These storms begin over the ocean. They can reach wind speeds of nearly 200 miles (320 kilometers) per hour as they reach shore. The state's deadliest hurricane was in 1999. That September, heavy rains from Hurricane Floyd caused many of the state's rivers to flood. The floods killed 52 people and caused about $6 billion in damage.

Forests and Wildlife

Forests cover nearly two-thirds of North Carolina. The state has four national forests. The two largest are the Nantahala National Forest and the Pisgah National Forest. Each forest covers more than 500,000 acres (202,000 hectares). Both forests are located in the Mountain Region.

Wildlife is plentiful in North Carolina. Deer, bats, opossums, and raccoons are common all over the state. River otters make their homes near the state's lakes, rivers, and streams. Black bears and bobcats roam the mountains

Wild Horses

Wild horses and ponies have roamed Currituck Banks and Ocracoke Island for more than 400 years. Some people believe the horses swam ashore from Spanish shipwrecks. Other people think early settlers brought the horses ashore.

Beginning in the 1950s, housing developments and paved roads destroyed much of the horses' habitat. In 1960, the National Park Service moved Ocracoke Island's 26 ponies to a 180-acre (73-hectare) range. In 1989, people in Corolla formed the Corolla Wild Horse Fund. These people moved most of the 100 horses to a large fenced area near the ocean. They moved others to an island in the Currituck Sound.

and the Coastal Plain. Reptiles and amphibians live in North Carolina's mild climate. Poisonous copperheads, rattlesnakes, and water moccasin snakes are native to the state.

Both freshwater and ocean fish thrive in North Carolina. The state's rivers and lakes are filled with trout, bass, walleye, bluegills, and sunfish. Marlin, sailfish, perch, mackerel, and other ocean fish swim near the Atlantic coast.

Explorer John White drew this picture of a North Carolina Indian village in the 1580s.

Chapter 3

History of North Carolina

European explorers reached present-day North Carolina in the 1500s. About 35,000 American Indians from about 30 tribes were living in the region. The Cherokee was the largest group. The Tuscarora and the Catawba were the other two major nations. Smaller tribes that belonged to the Algonquian Nation lived along North Carolina's northern coast. They were made famous in drawings by artist and explorer John White in the 1580s.

Early Exploration

Italian Giovanni da Verrazano was the earliest known European explorer of the North Carolina coast. He reached the Outer Banks in 1524.

In 1584, Queen Elizabeth I of England asked Sir Walter Raleigh to claim North American land for England. In 1585, Raleigh sent more than 100 men to Roanoke Island on the North Carolina coast. The settlers built the first English colony in America. They soon ran out of supplies. Most of the men returned to England in 1586. Only 15 men stayed on the island.

The Lost Colony

In 1587, John White led 117 English settlers to Roanoke Island. They planned to pick up the 15 men who stayed behind and travel north to Chesapeake Bay. The settlers found the skeleton of one of the men and no trace of the other 14. The ship's captain refused to travel any farther.

The settlers built a colony on the island, and White sailed back to England for supplies. A war between England and Spain kept him from returning until 1590. When he returned, White found empty houses and the word "CROATOAN" carved on a tree. The people had disappeared.

No one knows what happened to the Lost Colony. Some people believe a hurricane, Indians, or disease killed them. Others believe the colonists may have gone to live with the friendly Croatan Indians on another island. Some members of the Lumbee tribe of Robeson County and Coharie tribe of Sampson County claim to be descendants of the Croatan Indians and the vanished colonists.

Colonial Days

In 1629, the area that is now North and South Carolina was named in honor of King Charles I of England. It was called "The Province of Carolana," which means "The Land of

When John White returned to Roanoke Island, he found the word "CROATOAN" carved on a tree. All of the colonists had disappeared.

Charles." In a 1663 charter, King Charles II granted the land to eight wealthy Englishmen called the Lords Proprietors. The colony covered all of present-day North and South Carolina, northern Georgia, and all the land west of this area to the Pacific Ocean. The Proprietors chose governors to rule the colony and its people.

The first permanent white settlers in the northern part of the colony came from Virginia. They settled in the Albemarle Sound region around 1650. In 1705, people settled near the Pamlico River. The settlement became Bath, North Carolina's first town.

In 1712, the colony split into the colonies of North Carolina and South Carolina. In 1729, King George II bought the land from seven of the eight Proprietors' descendants. North Carolina became a British royal colony.

The Revolutionary War

By the 1760s, many people in North Carolina were unhappy with British Governor William Tryon's rule. In 1770, the Regulators rebelled against Tryon. This group was made up of farmers from the western Piedmont region of North Carolina. The governor's troops defeated the Regulators at the Battle of Alamance in May 1771.

German settlers built the town of Salem in 1766. Today, this town is part of Winston-Salem.

North Carolina patriots fought bravely at the Battle of Guilford Courthouse in 1781.

The Revolutionary War (1775–1783) began in April 1775. On May 20, 1775, colonists from Mecklenberg County met in Charlotte. Some people believe they wrote the Mecklenberg Declaration of Independence. On May 31, colonists in Mecklenberg County wrote the Mecklenberg Resolves. This document said that British laws did not apply to the colonists. It also set up a new self-government for the county.

On April 12, 1776, colonists met in Halifax to write the Halifax Resolves. In this document, the state's delegates to the Continental Congress agreed to vote for independence.

On July 4, 1776, all 13 colonies declared independence from Great Britain. Together they formed the United States of America. In December 1776, North Carolina adopted its first constitution. New Bern was the first capital.

Not everyone in North Carolina supported independence from Great Britain. Some people, called loyalists or Tories, wanted to remain under British rule. In 1776, North Carolina patriots defeated Tories at the Battle of Moore's Creek Bridge near Wilmington. In 1780, North Carolina patriots helped defeat Tories at the Battle of Kings Mountain. They fought just across the South Carolina border. In 1781, the British lost many soldiers, but won the Battle of Guilford Courthouse.

The British Army surrendered on October 19, 1781, at Yorktown, Virginia. In 1783, the Treaty of Paris officially ended the war.

North Carolina became the 12th state of the new Union on November 21, 1789. In 1792, Raleigh became the capital.

Progress in the 1800s

During the early 1800s, North Carolina had few factories, a poor transportation system, and no public schools. Its main industry was agriculture. Tobacco and cotton were the most important crops.

North Carolinians wanted to improve their state. In 1835, the state changed its constitution. The new constitution required the state to care for people who were disabled or mentally ill. In 1839, the state started a public school system.

Loss of the Cherokee

The Cherokee had lived in North Carolina for hundreds of years. They built towns and developed a written language.

By the 1820s, white settlers were moving onto Cherokee lands. The U.S. government passed laws that forced the Cherokee in the eastern states to move to what is now Oklahoma. In 1838, about 13,000 Cherokee joined a march to present-day Oklahoma. This march was known as the Trail of Tears. Thousands of Indians died during the journey. A small group of Cherokee hid in the Great Smoky Mountains. Some of their descendants still live there today.

The Civil War

By the 1850s, the issue of slavery divided the nation. Many Southerners believed they could not work their fields without slaves. They wanted to leave the Union and keep their slaves.

North Carolina supported the Union even after other Southern states seceded. But when the Civil War began,

North Carolinians refused to fight their fellow Southerners. On May 20, 1861, the state left the Union and joined the Confederate States of America. North Carolina sent more soldiers and supplies to the Confederacy than any other state. About 40,000 North Carolina soldiers died in the war. This number was the largest of any Confederate state. In 1865, the Union won the war, and the slaves were freed.

Reconstruction

During Reconstruction (1865–1877), the U.S. military governed North Carolina and other Southern states. Southern states had to write new constitutions. They had to give rights

In early 1865, Union General William Sherman led his soldiers through North Carolina. They burned towns, fields, and plantations as they moved through the state.

The Wright Brothers

North Carolina was the site of the first successful airplane flight. In 1900, brothers Orville and Wilbur Wright began testing gliders they had built. They did the testing at Kill Devil Hills, near the town of Kitty Hawk in North Carolina.

By 1903, the brothers had learned enough to build a gasoline-powered airplane. On December 17, 1903, Orville made the first successful flight with the airplane at Kill Devil Hills. The brothers tried several flights that day. On one of the flights, the airplane flew 120 feet (37 meters) before landing. Today, the site of the flight is now the Wright Brothers National Memorial.

to their African American citizens before the states could rejoin the Union. In 1868, North Carolina adopted a new constitution and rejoined the Union.

Many North Carolinians were angry that African Americans now had the same rights as white citizens. After Reconstruction ended, legislators changed the state's constitution to keep most African Americans from voting.

They passed laws that separated African Americans and whites. African Americans and whites were segregated in schools, restaurants, trains, streetcars, and other public places.

Changes in the 1900s

North Carolina's industries grew quickly after 1900. Wilmington's shipyards built ships for the U.S. Navy during World War I (1914–1918). By the late 1920s, North Carolina factories made more tobacco products, wooden furniture, and cotton textiles than any other state.

An improved transportation system also helped North Carolina's economy. Between 1921 and 1929, the state added about 7,500 miles (12,000 kilometers) of paved highways.

Hard Times and War

North Carolina's economy suffered during the Great Depression (1929–1939). Prices for factory goods fell and wages dropped. Businesses and banks closed. Factory workers lost their jobs, and farmers lost their land.

In 1941, the United States entered World War II (1939–1945). North Carolina mills and factories produced uniforms, parachutes, wood products, and aluminum for the war. Many North Carolinians found jobs in these factories.

"We cannot build a world-class workforce if our children don't come to school ready to learn. Too many children are coming to school ready to fail because we haven't reached them early enough. Those failures are North Carolina's failures. We can do better for our children, and we must."

—North Carolina Governor Jim Hunt, March 31, 1993

Civil Rights Issues

While North Carolina progressed, African Americans still suffered from discrimination. In 1954, the U.S. Supreme Court ruled that school segregation was illegal, but North Carolina's schools remained segregated.

African Americans began demanding fair treatment. On February 1, 1960, four African American students walked into a Woolworth store in Greensboro. They sat at the store's "white only" lunch counter. The students were refused service but remained seated. For several days, they returned and sat all day until the store agreed to serve people of all races.

The Civil Rights movement led the U.S. government to take action. Congress passed the Civil Rights Act in 1964. This law protects all U.S. citizens from discrimination. In fall 1965, limited integration began in many of the state's schools. In 1971, the U.S. Supreme Court ruled to integrate a North Carolina school district using all possible means. Children in Charlotte were bused from their neighborhoods to other schools.

Recent Events

After World War II ended, the North Carolina government worked to modernize the state. In 1959, the North Carolina Research Triangle Park opened between Raleigh and Durham. The area is a center for business and government research. It helped attract more industry to the state.

In 1993, Governor Jim Hunt began a program called Smart Start. The program provides money to improve child care and education for preschool children in the state. The program has won national awards and has been a model for programs in other states.

In February 1960, Joseph McNeil, Franklin McCain, Billy Smith, and Clarence Henderson protested segregation by sitting at a Greensboro lunch counter.

North Carolina's capitol is located in Union Square in Raleigh.

Chapter 4

Government and Politics

North Carolina adopted its first constitution in 1776. Under this constitution, the legislature, called the General Assembly, held all the power. The General Assembly chose all judges and state officials, including the governor. Only male property owners could vote for General Assembly members.

The first constitution was changed in 1835 and replaced in 1868. Property ownership was no longer required to vote. The executive branch of government was strengthened. The people elected the state's governor and judges. The governor's term was increased from one year to four years.

The current constitution was adopted in 1971. It gives North Carolinians more control of the state's government. For example, amendments can be proposed in the legislature.

Both the state senate and house of representatives must approve the suggested change. The voters then must approve the amendment in a general election.

Executive Branch

The head of North Carolina's executive branch is the governor. This branch includes the lieutenant governor and many state agencies. The people elect the governor and lieutenant governor. These officials serve four-year terms. They can serve no more than two terms in a row.

The governor appoints 10 state officials. These officials include the secretary of transportation and the secretary of commerce. This group is known as the governor's cabinet.

Voters elect the attorney general, state treasurer, secretary of state, and five other officials. These eight officials and the lieutenant governor make up the council of state. The council helps the governor make important decisions.

North Carolina's Government

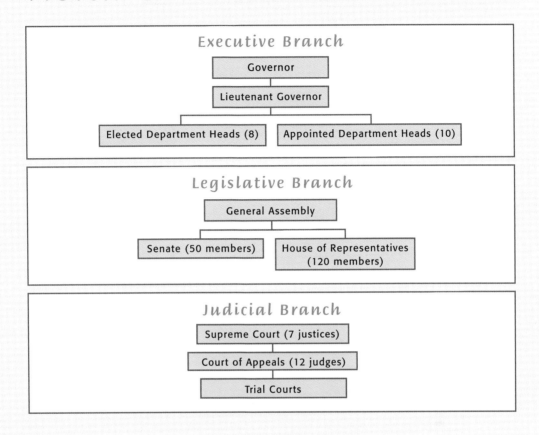

Executive Branch

Governor

Lieutenant Governor

Elected Department Heads (8)   Appointed Department Heads (10)

Legislative Branch

General Assembly

Senate (50 members)   House of Representatives (120 members)

Judicial Branch

Supreme Court (7 justices)

Court of Appeals (12 judges)

Trial Courts

Legislative Branch

The legislative branch writes and makes changes to the state's laws. The state's legislature is called the General Assembly. The General Assembly includes the senate and the house of representatives. The senate has 50 members. The house of representatives has 120 members. Both senators and representatives serve two-year terms.

Senator Jesse Helms

Jesse Helms was born in 1921 in Monroe, North Carolina. In 1972, Helms became the first Republican senator elected in North Carolina in more than 75 years.

Helms quickly became one of the country's most powerful politicians. From 1981 to 1987, he was chair of the Senate Committee on Agriculture, Nutrition, and Forestry. In 1995, he became chair of the Senate Foreign Relations Committee. He led this committee until 2001. Helms retired from the Senate in 2003.

Judicial Branch

North Carolina has three levels of courts. These courts are trial courts, the court of appeals, and the state supreme court.

Trial courts include district courts and superior courts. Cases that involve minor crimes and lawsuits are tried in district courts. Superior courts handle cases that involve more serious crimes.

People who do not agree with trial court decisions can take their cases to the court of appeals. After the court of appeals rules on the case, it may go before the state supreme court. The supreme court makes the final decision on all appealed cases.

North Carolinians elect the state's judges. The supreme court has a chief justice and six associate justices. The court of appeals has 12 judges. District court judges serve four-year terms. Supreme court justices and court of appeals judges serve eight-year terms.

State Politics

Democrats have controlled North Carolina politics throughout most of the state's history. In recent years, Republicans have made some gains in North Carolina. In 1972, North Carolinians elected their first Republican governor and U.S. senator since the 1890s. In 2002, North Carolinians elected Republican Elizabeth Dole to the U.S. Senate. Dole is North Carolina's first female U.S. senator.

North Carolina's farmers harvest more tobacco than farmers in any other state.

Chapter 5

Economy and Resources

For many years, North Carolina's economy depended on tobacco, cotton, and other crops. Today, manufacturing and service industries produce more income for the state than farming does.

Manufacturing

Manufacturing earns more money and provides more jobs than any other single industry in North Carolina. Medicines, cleaning products, fertilizers, and other chemical products earn the most money for the state. Tobacco products rank second. North Carolina factories make about half the cigarettes sold in the United States.

Textile mills provide the largest number of manufacturing jobs in the state. Textile products made in North Carolina include stockings, sheets and towels, and yarn. In recent years, some textile companies have closed their North Carolina plants. Some of these companies have opened plants in other countries, where labor costs are lower.

North Carolina produces more household furniture than any other state. Factories in Hickory, Lenoir, Lexington, Statesville, Thomasville, and other towns make wooden furniture. High Point is called the "Furniture Capital of America." Each April and October, High Point holds the world's largest wholesale home furnishings show.

Rubber products also are made in North Carolina. Kelly-Springfield's factory in Fayetteville is the largest tire factory in the world. Each day, it produces about 70,000 tires.

Service Industries

Education, health care, research, retail, and other service industries are a major part of North Carolina's economy.

This North Carolina furniture factory in Spruce Point is one of the state's many furniture factories. North Carolina produces much of the furniture sold in the United States.

Together, they make up nearly two-thirds of the total goods and services produced in the state.

Tourism and banking are among the state's largest service industries. More than 40 million tourists bring about

$12 billion to the state each year. North Carolina is the home of Bank of America, First Union, and Wachovia.

Several retail store chains have headquarters in North Carolina. In 1946, Jim Lowe and Carl Buchan opened Lowe's Hardware Store in North Wilkesboro. Today, the Lowe's chain of home improvement stores has more than 800 stores in the United States. The first Family Dollar discount store opened in Charlotte in 1959. The chain now operates more than 4,600 U.S. stores. The grocery store chain Food Lion has its headquarters in Salisbury. It has more than 1,200 stores in the eastern and southern United States.

Many North Carolina companies perform research. Research Triangle Park is the largest research park in the United States. More than 130 companies do research in electronics, medicines, and other areas. About 42,000 North Carolinians work at the park.

Agriculture

Agriculture has been a major part of North Carolina's economy since colonial times. Today, farmland covers about one-third of the state.

U.S. Military

IRON MIKE
IN HONOR OF
AIRBORNE TROOPERS
WHOSE COURAGE,
DEDICATION, AND
TRADITIONS MAKE THEM
THE WORLD'S FINEST
FIGHTING SOLDIERS

The U.S. military has had a major effect on North Carolina's economy since World War I. In 1918, the U.S. Army started building Camp Bragg near Fayetteville to train soldiers for the war. In 1922, Camp Bragg became Fort Bragg. Today, it is one of the largest military installations in the United States.

Other major military installations are located in North Carolina. Marines train at Camp Lejeune near Jacksonville and Cherry Point Marine Corps Air Station near Havelock. The Air Force has two bases in North Carolina. Pope Air Force Base is near Fayetteville. Seymour Johnson Air Force Base is near Goldsboro.

Livestock products provide most of the state's farm income. North Carolina produces more turkeys than any other state. The state is also one of the top producers of broiler chickens. Many hog farms are in the eastern part of the state. Only Iowa produces more hogs than North Carolina.

North Carolina farmers also grow crops. Tobacco is North Carolina's leading crop. North Carolina tops all states in tobacco production. Farmers also raise corn and soybeans for livestock feed. Cotton, peanuts, apples, peaches, and strawberries are other important crops.

Other farm products include greenhouse and nursery products, hay, trees, and wheat. North Carolina ranks second only to Oregon in Christmas tree production. The state's Christmas tree farms harvest about 4 million trees each year.

Mining and Fishing

North Carolina has deposits of more than 300 minerals and rocks. Quarries near Charlotte, Greensboro, and Raleigh produce limestone. Lithium compounds used to make

aluminum and glass are mined in the Piedmont. Phosphate rock from eastern North Carolina is used to make fertilizer.

North Carolina mines more feldspar, mica, and common clay than any other state. Much of the state's clay is made into pottery. The area near Seagrove and Sanford in central North Carolina is known for its pottery factories.

North Carolina's location on the Atlantic coast makes fishing an important industry. Much of the state's seafood is caught near the ports of Morehead City and Beaufort. Blue crab, king mackerel, and Atlantic croaker are caught off the North Carolina coast. The state's rivers, lakes, and fish farms are good sources of catfish and trout.

North Carolina Christmas tree farms, like this one in Ashe County, grow more Christmas trees each year than any state except Oregon.

North Carolina is known for its tasty food. The Snappy Lunch in Mount Airy is famous for its pork chop sandwich.

Chapter 6

People and Culture

North Carolina is the 11th most populated state in the country. Even with more than 8 million people, the state is less crowded than many other states. North Carolina's population is growing rapidly. The state's population grew 21 percent between 1990 and 2000. The U.S. population grew only 13 percent during the same period.

Ethnic Groups

Many North Carolinians are descendants of the state's first European settlers. The state has one of the largest Scots-Irish populations in the United States. Other North Carolinians have English or German backgrounds. During the late 1700s, many German immigrants who belonged to the Moravian Church came to North Carolina from Pennsylvania. They founded the town of Salem, which today is part of Winston-Salem. Many Moravians still live in that area today.

North Carolina has a large African American population. Most African Americans in North Carolina live in the Piedmont and the northern Coastal Plain.

North Carolina has the eighth largest American Indian population of all states. Yet the state's 100,000 American

The Cherokee drama, *Unto These Hills,* tells of the hardships of the Cherokee during the Trail of Tears. More history plays are performed in North Carolina than in any other state.

North Carolina's Ethnic Backgrounds

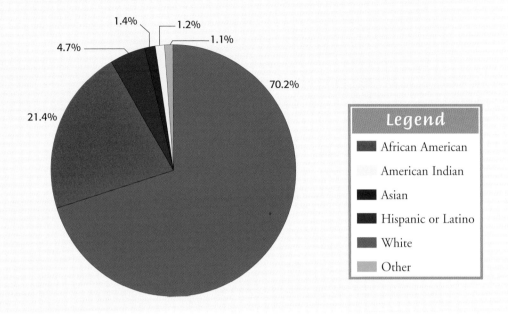

1.4%
1.2%
4.7%
1.1%
70.2%
21.4%

Legend
- African American
- American Indian
- Asian
- Hispanic or Latino
- White
- Other

Indians make up just slightly more than 1 percent of the state's population. About 40,000 Indians in North Carolina belong to the Lumbee tribe. Most Lumbee live in Robeson County. The Cherokee Indians form the second largest Indian group in North Carolina. Many Cherokee live on the Eastern Cherokee Reservation in the Great Smoky Mountains.

The state also is home to other ethnic groups. Almost 5 percent of the state's people are Hispanic. Many Asian Americans also live in the state. Fayetteville has a large Korean population.

Biltmore Estate

George Vanderbilt was the great-grandson of wealthy businessowner Cornelius Vanderbilt. In 1888, George Vanderbilt chose a site in the mountains of North Carolina to build a mansion he used as a summer home. The house was completed in 1895. Today, the Biltmore is still the largest private home in the world. The Biltmore has 250 rooms.

The Biltmore Estate is still owned by George Vanderbilt's family. Since 1930, it has been open to the public as a museum. Each year, 900,000 people visit the house and grounds.

Festivals

North Carolina offers a wide range of entertainment and recreation. Country music, fiddling, and folk dancing reflect the state's heritage and culture. The Mountain Dance and Folk Festival in Asheville and the Bluegrass and Old Time Fiddler's Convention in Mount Airy celebrate these traditional arts.

North Carolina cooks are famous for their barbecue. Shredded pork meat is covered with a tangy vinegar-based barbecue sauce. People enjoy barbecue at hog roasts called "pig pickings." As the hog roasts in an outdoor pit, people pick off pieces of the tasty meat. Each October, barbecue and music bring more than 100,000 people to the Barbecue Festival in Lexington.

Other festivals celebrate the state's ethnic backgrounds. Each summer, Lumbee Indians gather in Pembroke for the Lumbee Homecoming. This event includes traditional storytelling, music, and crafts. Scottish people celebrate their heritage at the Grandfather Mountain Highland Games.

Sports

North Carolinians enjoy playing and watching sports. Charlotte is the home of the Carolina Panthers NFL team. The Carolina Hurricanes play hockey in Raleigh. The Sting WNBA team plays in Charlotte. Soccer fans come to Cary to watch the Carolina Courage play. The University of North Carolina, North Carolina State University, and Duke University are known for their championship college basketball teams.

Car racing is popular in North Carolina. Charlotte, Asheville, Winston-Salem, Rockingham, and Wilkesboro have famous racetracks. Well-known racing families from North Carolina include the Earnhardts, the Pettys, and the Jarretts.

North Carolina's mild climate allows people to play golf nearly year-round. Each year, pro golf tournaments are held in the state. The Pinehurst Resort and Country Club in Moore County has been the site of major golf tournaments such as the U.S. Open.

A State of Progress

North Carolina is an appealing state with a pleasant climate, beautiful scenery, and wide range of activities. Today, North Carolina is becoming a state of progress. High-technology and research industries are replacing tobacco and textile industries. The state continues to work on giving its young people the best education possible.

As its nickname suggests, the Tar Heel State sticks to its challenges. Each struggle has helped North Carolina grow stronger and become a state with a bright future.

Race crews are busy at the many NASCAR races held every year at North Carolina Speedway in Rockingham.

Recipe: Pig-Picking Cake

This light, sweet cake goes well with North Carolina barbecue. Many people in North Carolina roast a whole pig in a charcoal cooker for a pig-picking party. This cake is a favorite dessert at pig-pickings.

Ingredients

1 tablespoon (15 mL) flour (to coat baking pan)
1 18.25-ounce (517-gram) package yellow cake mix without pudding
1 11-ounce (312-gram) can mandarin oranges, undrained
4 eggs
½ cup (120 mL) vegetable oil
1 20-ounce (567-gram) can crushed pineapple, drained
1 8-ounce (227-gram) container non-dairy whipped topping
1 3.4-ounce (96-gram) package vanilla instant pudding

Equipment

9- by 13-inch (23-by 33-centimeter) baking pan
measuring spoons
nonstick cooking spray
2 medium-size bowls
electric mixer
toothpick
oven mitts
rubber spatula

What you do

1. Preheat oven to 350°F (180°C).

2. Spray inside of baking pan with nonstick cooking spray. Sprinkle flour into pan. Shake the sides of the pan until the entire inside of the pan is coated with flour. Shake out any excess flour into the garbage can.

3. Combine cake mix, mandarin oranges, eggs, and vegetable oil in bowl. With electric mixer, beat 2 minutes at high speed. Beat 1 minute more at low speed.

4. Pour cake mixture into baking pan. Bake 25 to 30 minutes or until a toothpick inserted in center of the cake comes out clean.

5. Use oven mitts to take pan out of oven. Cool cake for 1 hour.

6. In second bowl, combine pineapple, whipped topping, and pudding. Beat 2 minutes at medium speed with mixer. Let mixture stand 5 minutes.

7. Use spatula to spread whipped topping mixture over cake. Chill in refrigerator at least 2 hours before serving.

8. Store cake in the refrigerator.

Makes 18 servings

North Carolina's Flag and Seal

North Carolina's Flag

North Carolina adopted its flag in 1885. The flag's right side is red on the top and white on the bottom. The left side is dark blue with a white star separating the letters N and C. A ribbon above the star shows the date of the Mecklenberg Declaration of Independence. A ribbon beneath the star has the date of the Halifax Resolves.

North Carolina's State Seal

North Carolina adopted its seal in 1893. The seal is round, with the goddesses Liberty and Plenty in the center. Liberty stands for freedom. Plenty represents agriculture. Mountains, plains, coastline, and a ship fill the background. They represent the state's history and landscape. The date of the Mecklenberg Declaration of Independence is at the top of the seal. The date of the Halifax Resolves is at the bottom of the seal. The state motto, "esse quam videri," is at the bottom. The motto means "to be, rather than to seem."

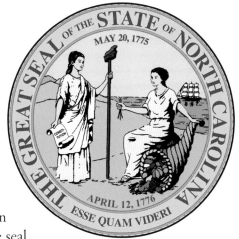

Almanac

Nickname: Tar Heel State

Population: 8,049,313 (U.S. Census, 2000)
Population rank: 11th

Capital: Raleigh

Largest cities: Charlotte, Raleigh, Greensboro, Durham, Winston-Salem

Agricultural products: Poultry, tobacco, pork, greenhouse products, beef, soybeans

Average summer temperature: 76 degrees Fahrenheit (24 degrees Celsius)

Average winter temperature: 42 degrees Fahrenheit (6 degrees Celsius)

Average annual precipitation: 49 inches (124 centimeters)

Area: 53,821 square miles (139,396 square kilometers)
Size rank: 29th

Highest point: Mount Mitchell, 6,684 feet (2,037 meters)

Lowest point: Atlantic Ocean, sea level

cardinal

dogwood

Symbols

Bird: Cardinal

Dog: Plott hound

Flower: Dogwood

Gemstone: Emerald

Insect: Honeybee

Economy

Natural resources: Phosphate rock, sand, gravel, clay, feldspar, kaolin, limestone, shale, lithium, timber

Types of industry: Chemicals, tobacco products, textiles, furniture, mining, fishing, tourism

Symbols

Mammal: Eastern gray squirrel

Song: "The Old North State" by William Gaston and Mrs. E. E. Randolph

Tree: Pine

Government

First governor: Richard Caswell

Statehood: November 21, 1789 (12th state)

U.S. Representatives: 13

U.S. Senators: 2

U.S. electoral votes: 15

Counties: 100

Timeline

State History

1524
About 35,000 American Indians are living in North Carolina when Giovanni da Verrazano explores the mouth of the Cape Fear River.

1705
People settle near the Pamlico River in a settlement that becomes Bath, which is North Carolina's first town.

1868
North Carolina rejoins the United States of America.

1590
John White finds Roanoke Colony deserted.

1789
North Carolina becomes the 12th state.

U.S. History

1620
The Pilgrims establish a colony in the New World.

1775–1783
American colonists and the British fight the Revolutionary War.

1861–1865
The Union and the Confederacy fight the Civil War.

1903

The Wright brothers make the first successful powered airplane flight at Kitty Hawk.

1999

Cape Hatteras Lighthouse is moved; Hurricane Floyd kills 52 people and causes $6 billion in damage.

1918

Camp Bragg opens near Fayetteville; it later becomes Fort Bragg.

1959

Research Triangle Park opens near Durham.

1960

Four African Americans hold a sit-in after they are refused service at a lunch counter in Greensboro.

1929–1939

The United States experiences the Great Depression.

2001

On September 11, terrorists attack the World Trade Center and the Pentagon.

1914–1918

World War I is fought; the United States enters the war in 1917.

1939–1945

World War II is fought; the United States enters the war in 1941.

1964

U.S. Congress passes the Civil Rights Act, which makes any form of discrimination illegal.

Words to Know

cape (KAPE)—a part of the coastline that extends into the ocean

civil rights (SIV-il RITES)—the rights that all people have to freedom and equal treatment under the law

Confederacy (kuhn-FED-ur-uh-see)—the group of 11 Southern states that declared independence from the United States in 1860 and 1861

hurricane (HUR-uh-kane)—a strong wind and rain storm that starts on the ocean

integration (in-tuh-GRAY-shuhn)—the process of bringing people of all races together in schools and other public places

pottery (POT-uh-ree)—objects made of baked clay or the places where these objects are made

secede (si-SEED)—to formally withdraw from a group or organization; the Confederate states seceded from the United States at the time of the Civil War.

segregation (seg-ruh-GAY-shuhn)—the practice of keeping people of different races apart

sound (SOUND)—a long, narrow area of water between two other bodies of water or between the mainland and an island

textile (TEK-stile)—thread, yarn, or cloth that has been woven or knitted

To Learn More

Dolan, Edward F. *The Lost Colony of Roanoke.* Kaleidoscope. New York: Benchmark Books, 2002.

Shirley, David. *North Carolina.* Celebrate the States. New York: Benchmark Books, 2001.

Sullivan, George. *The Wright Brothers.* In Their Own Words. New York: Scholastic Reference, 2002.

Weintraub, Aileen. *Cape Hatteras Light: The Tallest Lighthouse in the United States.* Great Lighthouses of North America. New York: PowerKids Press, 2002.

Internet Sites

Do you want to find out more about North Carolina?
Let FactHound, our fact-finding hound dog, do the research for you!

Here's how:

1) Visit ***http://www.facthound.com***
2) Type in the **Book ID** Number:
   0736821902
3) Click on **FETCH IT.**

FactHound will find Internet sites picked by our editors just for you!

Places to Write and Visit

Biltmore Estate
One North Pack Square
Asheville, NC 28801

Cape Hatteras National Seashore
1401 National Park Drive
Manteo, NC   27954

North Carolina Division of Tourism, Film, and Sports Development
301 North Wilmington Street
Raleigh, NC 27601

North Carolina Museum of History
5 East Edenton Street
4650 Mail Service Center
Raleigh, NC 27699-4650

Pisgah National Forest
Pisgah Ranger District
1001 Pisgah Highway
Pisgah Forest, NC   28768

Research Triangle Foundation of North Carolina
2 Hanes Drive
P.O. Box 12255
Research Triangle Park, NC 27709

The Seagrove area of North Carolina is famous for its pottery.

Index

African Americans, 28–29, 30, 31, 48–49
agriculture, 10, 26, 38, 39, 42–44
American Indians, 18, 19, 21, 26, 48–49
Atlantic Coastal Plain, 9–10, 14–15, 17, 48
Atlantic Ocean, 5, 6, 14

banks, 29, 41–42

Cape Hatteras Lighthouse, 4, 6
Charles I, King, 21–22
Charles II, King, 22
Christmas tree farms, 44, 45
Civil Rights, 30, 31
Civil War, 26–27
climate, 15–16, 17, 53
Confederate soldiers, 6, 27

Democrats, 37
Dismal Swamp, 9

education, 25, 26, 30, 31, 40, 53
Elizabeth I, Queen, 20
executive branch, 34

festivals, 50–51
flag, 55
floods, 16
forests, 16
Fort Bragg, 43

government, 33–37

Grandfather Mountain, 12–13

horses, 17
hurricanes, 16

judicial branch, 36

Kill Devil Hills, 28
Kitty Hawk, 28

lakes, 15, 16, 17, 45
legislative branch, 35
livestock, 43, 44
Lost Colony, 20–21

manufacturing, 39–40
Mecklenberg Declaration of Independence, 24, 55
Mecklenberg Resolves, 24
minerals, 44–45
Mountain Region, 10, 12–13, 15, 16
mountains, 12, 13, 14, 26
Mount Mitchell, 12

National Park Service, 6, 17

Outer Banks, 5, 19

Piedmont, 9, 10, 15, 23
pirates, 5
population, 47
precipitation, 15

Raleigh, Sir Walter, 20

Reconstruction, 27–29
recreation, 50–51
Republicans, 36, 37
Research Triangle Park, 31, 42
Revolutionary War, 23–25
rivers, 10, 14–15, 16, 17, 22, 45

Sandhills, 10
seal, 55
segregation, 29, 30, 31
Sherman, General William 27
shipwrecks, 5, 17
slavery, 26–27
sports, 51–53

Tar Heel, 6, 53
textiles, 29, 40, 53
tobacco, 26, 29, 38, 39, 43, 44, 53
tourism, 41
Trail of Tears, 26, 48
transportation, 25, 29

Verrazano, Giovanni da, 19
voting, 25, 28, 33, 34

war, 6, 20, 23–25, 26–27, 29, 31, 43
White, John, 18, 19–21
wildlife, 16–17
World War I, 29, 43
World War II, 29, 31
Wright Brothers, 28